BELWIN CONTEST WINNERS

12 Original Piano Solos from the Libraries of Belwin-Mills and Summy-Birchard

Foreword

Exciting piano solos are motivating for students, as well as thrilling for audiences. Thoughtfully written and carefully graded original compositions are essential for every piano studio and produce successful learning experiences for students.

Over the years Belwin-Mills and Summy-Birchard produced extensive libraries of quality elementary and intermediate supplementary piano music. The pieces that are included in this series represent the two companies' most popular and effective solos drawn from festival and contest lists. Divided into four graded collections, outstanding works are made available again by Gilbert Allen, Stephen Burch, Hazel Cobb, Olive Dungan, Bernice Frost, Louise Garrow, Jon George, William L. Gillock, David Carr Glover, Roger Grove, Martha Mier, Mark Nevin, Walter Noona, Lynn Freeman Olson, Charles Donald Porter, Betty Sutton, Robert D. Vandall, Mary Verne, and June Weybright. Their time-tested solos are found on the following pages in approximate order of difficulty.

Contents

Produced by
Alfred Music Publishing Co., Inc.
P.O. Box 10003
Van Nuys, CA 91410-0003
alfred.com

Printed in USA.

ISBN-10: 0-7390-9280-4
ISBN-13: 978-0-7390-9280-4

SPANISH SERENADE

Lynn Freeman Olson

THE VIKING

Walter Noona

To Alice Gray Harrison

AEOLIAN HARP

William L. Gillock

Moderately slowly; somewhat freely

use soft pedal throughout

CEREMONIAL

Lynn Freeman Olson

REFLECTIONS OF THE MOON

Olive Dungan

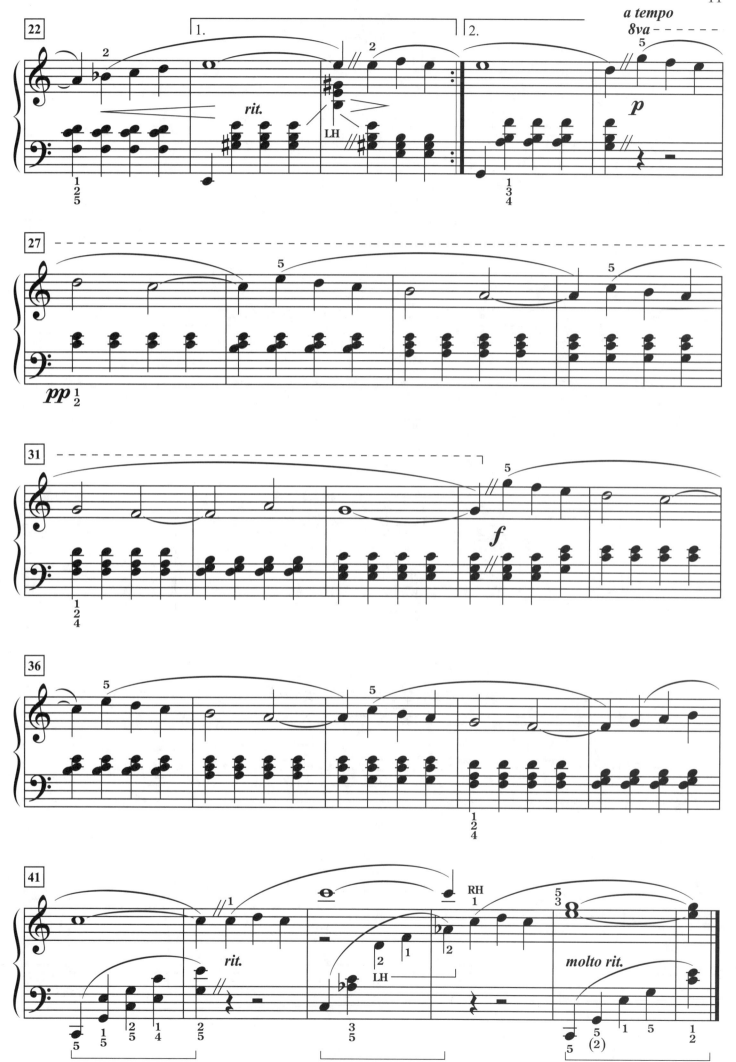

HOPAK

Mark Nevin

* Right hand may be played one octave higher if desired.

THE SPIDER DANCE

Walter Noona

COFFEE BEANS

Walter Noona

¡OLÉ!

Lynn Freeman Olson

SHADOWS ON THE MOON

Louise Garrow

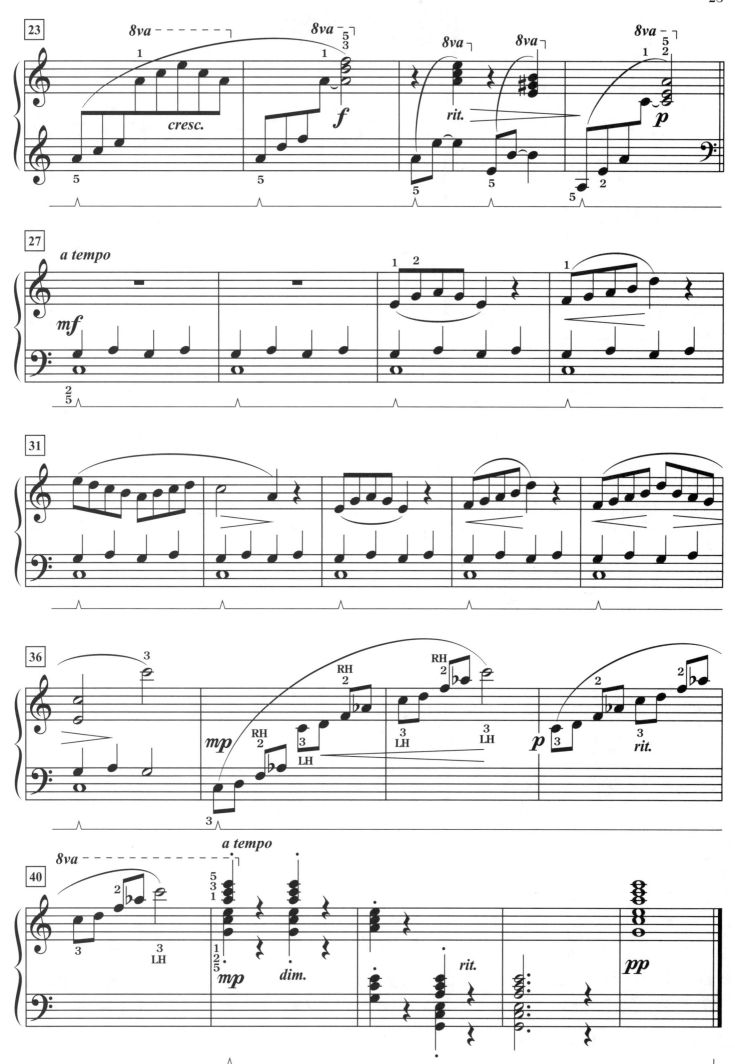

SONATINA IN A MINOR

I

Hazel Cobb

II

III
Rondo

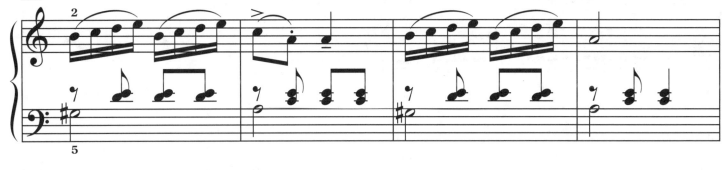

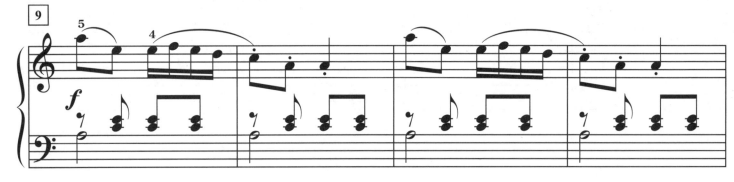

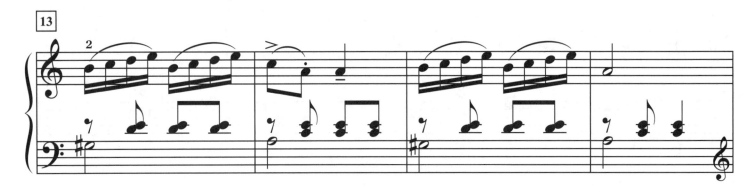

BRAZILIANA

June Weybright

D.S. al Fine

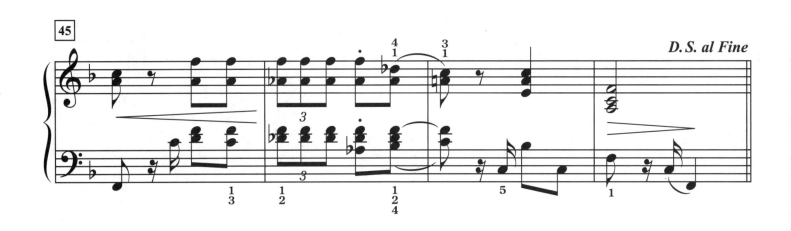